NATIONAL GEOGRAPHIC
KiDS

CRITTER CHAT

WORLD WiLD WEB

What if ANIMALS used SOCIAL MEDIA?

JASON VIOLA

NATIONAL GEOGRAPHIC
Washington, D.C.

Hey! My friends call me **FastClass.** Thanks to the internet, I get to chat with my pals from all around the world—even when we're on different continents! But I'm usually in too much of a rush to stick around. As a cheetah, I can go from **0 to 60 miles an hour** (97 km/h) in just **three seconds.** Can you make it to the end of this book before me? **Gotta run!**

CRITTER CHAT

HUMPHEAD WRASSE
SCREEN NAME: HatHead
CHAT TOPIC: Reef Defenders

FRIENDS

StillSanding
Parrotfish

TinyTube
Tunicate

ClamBoss
Giant clam

...

HatHead
Happy New Year, everybody! Who's got resolutions? *#NewYearNewMe*

StillSanding
I resolve to add a couple hundred pounds (100 kg) of sand to the beach.

TinyTube
Sand?! Good luck with that!

StillSanding
I don't need luck when I've got teeth inside my throat! I grind coral skeletons into beautiful poops of white sand.

TURN PAGE
● ● ●

HatHead
This year, I'm going to eat a ton of starfish! *#NomNom*

TinyTube
Resolutions are supposed to be about self-improvement.

HatHead
Outbreaks of crown of thorns starfish are devastating to coral reefs! Eating them keeps things under control. *#WorldPeace*

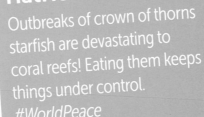

TinyTube
As an immobile invertebrate filter-feeder, I do my part by consuming bacteria and purifying the water. But you don't see me making a resolution about it.

TinyTube
I startle easily, shooting water at anything that gets too close. This year, I'd like to relax and appreciate life attached to this mollusk shell.

ClamBoss
YOU MEAN MY SHELL?

TinyTube
I just did a spit-take. *#YearRuined*

StillSanding
Don't type in all caps, ClamBoss. It looks like you're shouting.

ClamBoss
AS A 500-POUND (227-kg) CLAM, I TYPE HOW I WANT.

llama**zon**
the **BEAST** place to shop

den deodorizer

Toilet Air Freshener

My latrine has **never** smelled so good.

CUSTOMER REVIEWS

★★★★☆ **One spray will keep the stink away!**

Badger Verified Customer

My sense of smell is 800 times stronger than a human's, so bathroom smells are really noticeable. Even though my family's latrine pit is outside our burrow, sometimes you need a little help with the funk! We also change our grass and leaves frequently, and this product keeps everything smelling fresh.

10

Dolphinstagram

yellowhead_jawfish
📍 Caribbean Sea

SELFIE!

❤️ **54 likes**

yellowhead_jawfish Jawfish are master burrow builders! I used my big mouth to scoop up sand and create a tunnel. I even decorated the entrance with little pebbles. I'm a total homebody. Plus, it's always good to have a place to hide if a predator swims too close!!
#TakeCover #DIY #HomeImprovement

11

YiPadvisor

Two wings way up!

roseate_spoonbill
Cancun, Mexico

Member for 4 years

OMG, our trip to Cancun was amazing! So many cool hotels and beaches. It was like an all-you-can-eat buffet at every place we stopped. I can't tell you how many crustaceans and fish I devoured! All the carotenoids in them made my feathers SUPER pink. I've never looked better. I highly recommend it for my fellow spoonbill fashionistas!

ANIMAL INFLUENCER

ESTHER
THE WONDER PIG

SPECIES
Pig

FAVORITE FOODS
Hay, special kibble made for pigs, fruits, and vegetables

WHY SHE'S POPULAR
She's got a BIG personality.

In 2012, Steve Jenkins and Derek Walter thought they were adopting a rescued micro pig. Also known as teacup pigs, these animals usually don't get bigger than 70 pounds (32 kg). But Esther just kept growing and growing!

She now weighs between 500 and 600 pounds (227 and 272 kg)—about as much as a grizzly bear! Even though she turned out to be a much bigger pet than they planned for, Steve and Derek were charmed by Esther's colorful personality and curious nature. She soon gained fame as "Esther the Wonder Pig" on social media.

Esther and her owners use their popularity to talk about animal activism and bring awareness to how commercial farms treat animals. In some places, there are no laws or rules to protect these animals from mistreatment.

In 2014, Esther's followers helped make Happily Ever Esther Farm Sanctuary a reality. It provides a safe home for rescued or abandoned farm animals. Residents at the sanctuary include pigs, cows, goats, chickens, rabbits, sheep, a donkey, and a horse.

Pigs can be **HOUSEBROKEN!** Like dogs, pet pigs can let people know when they need to go potty outside and come back in.

Pigs' snouts are **VERY FLEXIBLE,** allowing them to **ROOT OUT** food from the ground.

Pigs are very **SMART ANIMALS** that love to **ROOT, PLAY,** and **EAT!**

yowl

I'd fly back anytime!

Nile Crocodile's Teeth
Egyptian_plover

★★★★★

When my friend first suggested lunch in a crocodile's mouth, I was like, "Rain check?!" But, let me tell you, this was a fantastic dining experience. The mouth was huge, so my friend and I had a lot of room AND the portions were impressive. I did not leave hungry! It's true we had to do some work to get the meat out from between the teeth, but it was worth it. We especially enjoyed the buffalo. I'll definitely be back.

Dolphinstagram

Glaucus_atlanticus
📍 Atlantic Ocean

 261 likes

Glaucus_atlanticus I'm a small, stylish sea slug who floats on the ocean surface. I've got two color options for camouflage. My blue side faces up so it blends in with the blue water, and my silvery side faces down and shimmers like sunlight. This glamour is perfect for confusing any predators. #WildStyleInspo #FashionANDFunction

17

CRITTER CHAT

PUMA

SCREEN NAME:
BradleyCougar

CHAT TOPIC: Big Cat Club

FRIENDS

HotSpot
Leopard

SpottySignal
Jaguar

FastClass
Cheetah

TURN PAGE

HotSpot
Greetings from sub-Saharan Africa! Just resting while I wait for nightfall.

BradleyCougar
I don't blame you. Night is the best time to ambush a deer.

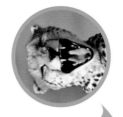

FastClass
no time 2 chat gotta go sry

BradleyCougar
Slow down, FastClass. You're always running off!

SpottySignal
Who needs speed when you've got strength? Last night I crunched a crocodile's skull with one bite!

HotSpot
I'm more of a gazelle kind of cat. Aren't crocs usually in the water?

SpottySignal
I love the water! The Amazon rainforest has lots of good places for a quick dip. Really clears my head. #SwimLife

20

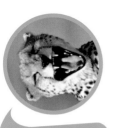

FastClass
Ugh! I was just about to feast on a nice antelope when some random hyenas snatched it away!
Has this happened to anyone else?

BradleyCougar
Don't know any hyenas but that's super rude.

HotSpot
I dragged mine up a tree so those scavengers can't get it.

SpottySignal
Props for that, HotSpot. A whole antelope!

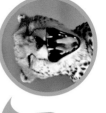

FastClass
Got 2 run C u later.

CRAFTY
COMMUNICATOR

ravens

What do babies do when they want to draw your attention to something? They point! Gesturing to an object is an important milestone in human communication. And ravens are the first nonprimates to be seen making gestures.

If another raven is watching (and especially if it's the opposite sex), a raven might pick up a stone or twig in its beak as if to say, "Hey, look at this cool thing I found!" The items aren't food and they're not for nest-building. Researchers think the purpose may be to interact and bond—kind of like starting a conversation with someone new you've met.

Like any family, raven families can invent their own names for things. As couples defend their territory and raise nestlings together, they develop their own calls, whose meanings are unique to them. Does your family have a special name for anything?

Raven calls sound **GURGLED** and **CROAKY,** compared to a crow's distinct **CAW!**

SMARTER than most mammals, ravens **PLAN** ahead, **USE TOOLS,** and **TRICK** one another.

Scientists believe ravens **MATE FOR LIFE.**

Dolphinstagram

Oriental_dwarf_kingfisher

📍 Southeast Asia

SELFIE!

❤️ **273 likes**

Oriental_dwarf_kingfisher At only five inches (12.7 cm) tall, I'm one of the smallest members of the kingfisher species. But don't be fooled: I'm a serious hunter. Here's my secret: If I catch a tiny, squirming lizard, I hold it in my beak and smash it against a stone until it relents. It's simple, but it works. Don't underestimate the little guys!
#HuntingTips #SmallButFierce

DANCE DANCE EVOLUTION

@peacock_spider

♫ "Single Ladies" • by Beyoncé

Welcome new followers! Thank you SO MUCH for watching my videos. I change up the music, but my moves are classic—I hop up and down, raise my legs up high, and lift my colorful tail-flap for an extra pop of drama. My videos are for everyone, but I'm REALLY looking for a special someone. If you think that's you, let me know in the comments!

200

66

CRITTER CHAT

SPOTTED SKUNK
SCREEN NAME: SprayDaze
CHAT TOPIC: Stink_o_Stank

FRIENDS

Rank_and_Foul
Musk ox

PUtiful
Hoatzin

StenchKing
Beaver

...

StenchKing
Been working all night gathering stones and cutting wood for the second den in our family lodge. Thank goodness my teeth are reinforced with iron! *#HomeImprovement*

PUtiful
A second den? La-dee-da! *#Fancy*

StenchKing
One's for entering and drying off, but the second room has a sturdy floor. It's where we sleep and take care of the kits.

Rank_and_Foul
You could just grow two coats of fur like me. An undercoat will keep you dry and warm.

TURN PAGE

StenchKing
Not looking for advice, but thanks.

SprayDaze
Tonight was a lot for me, too! I had to spray two foxes, two coyotes, and a golden retriever! I need a week to recover.

Rank_and_Foul
Seriously? I use MY odor to mark my territory. Why are you spraying other animals?

PUtiful
Seems rude.

SprayDaze
Don't worry, guys, I warn them first.

Rank_and_Foul
It better be a good warning.

 **SprayDaze**
I do a handstand.
Hotcha!

 SELFIE!

PUtiful
And if they don't leave?

 **SprayDaze**
I ruin their day with a good stinky spray!

amazon
the *BEAST* place to shop

best rodent soap

Bar of Soap

Better options are out there!

CUSTOMER REVIEWS

★ ★ ☆ ☆ ☆ **Sand is better**

Mongolian_gerbil Verified Customer

I might get a lot of haters for this, but I think sand is way better for washing than soap and water. Now hear me out—sand is awesome at getting debris off your fur if you roll around in it. And your coat will be shinier and smoother, too. Water just leaves you ... wet. And soap leaves a weird residue. No thank you.

Dolphinstagram

superb_lyrebird
📍 Southeast coast of Australia

 650 likes

superb_lyrebird As a male lyrebird, I've got an elegant tail, which I flash during courtship displays. And I'm a great singer. I can imitate sounds made by other birds, animals, and humans. I've even been able to mimic car alarms. If you've got it, flaunt it. #SelfLove #TooMuchTalentForOneBird #MimicGoals

Dolphinstagram

mole
📍 North America

 26 likes

mole It's just another day in the life for this underground foodie! I spend most of my time digging tunnels to find worms and grubs living in the dirt. It's a lot of work, so I need to eat 70–100 percent of my weight in bugs every day. Humans often complain that my constant digging ruins their lawns, gardens, and golf courses. #Oops

CRITTER CHAT

ROOSTER

SCREEN NAME: CombAlone
CHAT TOPIC: Farm Life

NobodysFoal
Shetland pony

GhostFace
Barn owl

OinkoBoinko
Pig

FRIENDS

4:16 a.m.

CombAlone
GOOD MORNING, EVERYBODY!
GOOD MORNING!!!!

OinkoBoinko
Ugh, enough. The sun's not even up!

CombAlone
Doesn't have to be. I've got an internal clock that says it's officially ... MORNING! GOOD MORNING!!! #RiseAndShine

OinkoBoinko
We're not on Rooster Time. Nobody wants to hear your racket!

GhostFace
I've been up all night. I don't give a hoot.

NobodysFoal
But you're an owl. You always give a hoot!

GhostFace
Not barn owls. We give a screech.

SELFIE!

NobodysFoal
I trotted right into that one.

36

GhostFace
I shriek to invite female owls over to my nest.

CombAlone
GOOD MORNING!!
GOOD MORNING!!
GOOD MORNING!!

GhostFace
SCREEEEEEEEEECH!!

OinkoBoinko
Where's the snooze button?

Komodo National Park
komodo_dragon
★★★★☆ ✓

This is the best park in Indonesia, CLAWS DOWN. Want tropical rainforests? Check! How about grass–woodland savannas? Got 'em! Looking for pristine white sandy beaches? Got those too! But here's the best part: more than 2,000 komodo dragons! The only reason I didn't give it 5 stars is all the tourists. At least they keep their distance. They must know I can run and swim up to 13 miles an hour (23 km/h) and have excellent vision for tracking prey.

Thisssss issss the bessst place!

CreamPuff

SPECIES: Pufferfish
LIKES: Algae, invertebrates, swims at sunset
DISLIKES: Humans, surprises, sharing territory with other fish

ABOUT ME: I'm looking for a female pufferfish who appreciates elaborate romantic gestures. I'm one of those guys who will take the time to sculpt designs in the sand on the seafloor for a special lady. It can take seven to nine days to complete, but I'm willing to commit if you are!

39

JUNIPER FOXX

SPECIES
North American red fox

FAVORITE FOODS
Some raw meats, small amounts of fruits and vegetables

WHY SHE'S POPULAR
That happy smile

Juniper Foxx and her owner, Jessika Coker, live with a group of other rescued exotic animals in Florida. She is considered a "ranched fox," which means she is descended from animals that were originally bred for their fur, and she has never lived in the wild.

Ranched foxes don't have all the natural instincts needed to survive on their own. Most domesticated animals need humans to feed them and keep them healthy.

That doesn't mean she's completely tame! Juniper is "wild mannered," so she still has a lot of traits and behaviors typical of wild foxes. For example, foxes mark their territories and valuables with their scent. Their urine and feces have very strong odors. Foxes are also good diggers, so they can quickly destroy flooring in a house or escape from a fenced backyard.

With three million followers and counting, Juniper and Friends are a hit on social media, where their owner shows off cute pictures of the animals' daily lives. Jessika also teaches people about the challenges of caring for exotic animals. They are different from cats and dogs and often don't make good pets. That's why "wild-mannered" pets like Juniper are best left to the experts—and for getting to know online!

Fox **HABITATS** are underground burrows called **DENS,** or **EARTHS.**

Foxes are **NOCTURNAL ANIMALS,** meaning they are most active during the night.

Foxes use their **HEARING** to find and **POUNCE** on insects and small mammals.

CRITTER CHAT

ORANGUTAN

SCREEN NAME: SwingTime
CHAT TOPIC: Confession Booth

FRIENDS

Staredown
Shoebill

MortalWombat
Wombat

Pira-NOT
Pacu

Pira-NOT
Some see my strong jaws and think I eat like a piranha. But I'm mostly vegetarian. *#RealTalk*

SwingTime
No shame from me. I love eating plants, especially fruit! My favorite is durian.

Staredown
Ouch! That looks sharp.

SwingTime
I use a leaf to protect my hand when I crack one open. It smells like raw sewage. *Mmm.*

Pira-NOT
You know, sometimes the smelliest foods are the tastiest. I'd try it!

TURN PAGE
• • •

Staredown
It was a really hot day today, and I pooped all over my legs and feet.

MortalWombat
It happens now and then. Don't sweat it.

Staredown
I can't sweat—that's why I did it! There's no cooler feeling than standing covered in your own poop.

SwingTime
You do you!

Staredown
I'm so glad we can all talk without any judgment. #SafeSpace

MortalWombat
So, I've told you before that I use my butt to block my burrow entrance.

 **SwingTime**
Still sounds risky to me, but go on.

MortalWombat
Last night a dingo chased me inside before I could block the entrance—so I used my butt to crush that predator against the wall.

 Staredown
That sounds like a close call! It didn't try to bite you?

 **MortalWombat**
Meh. I can take it. #BunsOfSteel

CRAFTY COMMUNICATOR

reef squid

Imagine if your skin turned a sparkly purple every time you felt nervous ... or a bright gold color if you got scared. Then you'd have a lot in common with reef squid! Reef squid communicate by changing the color of their skin.

Squid change their appearance by using cells underneath the surface of their skin that contain sacs of pigment. Most of the time, these sacs look like tiny dots on the squid's skin. But when a squid needs to change color, the sacs expand, becoming vibrant orange, red, and yellow in the process. Reef squid use colored patterns as camouflage from predators, even hiding in open water by mimicking the light reflected on the ocean's surface.

Like a lot of other animals, color plays an important part when squid look for mates. When he's ready to mate, a male turns red to attract a female and white to warn away other males. As he swims alongside a female, he'll split the colors right down the middle, turning red on her side and white on the opposite side. We're not squiddin' you!

Octopuses and cuttlefish also **CHANGE COLOR.**

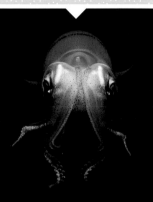

Reef squid can **JUMP SIX FEET** (2 m) above the water and **"FLY" 32 FEET** (10 m) through the air.

Squid shoot **CLOUDS** of **DARK INK** to confuse predators.

Dolphinstagram

markhor
📍 Pakistan

SELFIE!

❤️ **103 likes**

markhor Sometimes I feel like I was born to climb, and that's because I was! My hooves are wide, so they're great for navigating tricky terrain. Don't worry about the massive spiraling horns on my head—I can balance with them just fine. They even come in handy when I need to intimidate other males during mating season. #BeastMode #NeverStopClimbing

52

Teamwork **makes the dream work.**

YiPadvisor

olive_baboon
Elephant caravan in East Africa

Member for 2 years

Quick travel tip: If your troop is ever searching for water, these elephants are lifesavers. For real. They can find underground water and dig out wells in all kinds of places. It's so cool to watch! In exchange for the refreshing drinks, the elephants expect you to let them know if any predators are lurking around. My troop didn't mind. The cool shade of the treetops made a fine lookout point!

CRITTER CHAT

SUN BEAR
SCREEN NAME: SolarBear
CHAT TOPIC: Bears Only

FRIENDS

ClawfulGood
Tardigrade

HoneyHabit
Kinkajou

KoaltyTime
Koala

SolarBear
Just finished off a night of foraging and want to wind down before I turn in. Any bear buds around to chat?

HoneyHabit
I'm about to log off. I'm brushing pollen off my face after a nice nectar drink before nodding off in my tree. *#Daydreaming*

KoaltyTime
As a koala bear, I'm always up for a nap! I sometimes sleep 18 hours in a day.

ClawfulGood
I can sleep for several years at a time if I have to.

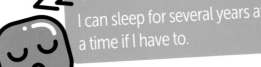

TURN PAGE

SolarBear
Most of us are no strangers to hibernation, but I've never heard of a bear who can sleep so long!

ClawfulGood
A super-sleep state called "cryptobiosis" allows water bears like me to survive dehydration, extreme cold, and even cosmic radiation! We were the first bears in space.

SolarBear
Slow down. Where do you live?

ClawfulGood
Me? A patch of moss in a parking lot. But water bears can live anywhere there's water, basically.

SolarBear
Then how come I've never seen you before?

ClawfulGood
Probably because we're microscopic.

HoneyHabit
You don't sound like a bear.

ClawfulGood
But I have little bear claws! Four pairs.

TURN PAGE

5:45 a.m.

SolarBear
Every bone in my body says you're not a bear.

ClawfulGood
Not sure what that feels like. I don't have any bones in my body.

HoneyHabit
It's cool. I'm not really a bear either. They just call me "honey bear" because I like to raid beehives.

SolarBear
Ugh, this group is supposed to be #BearsOnly!

58

KoaltyTime
I feel you, SolarBear. It's just so hard to trust anyone online.

SolarBear
It is!

KoaltyTime
I'm raising a joey in my pouch and I worry what kind of world she's entering.

SELFIE!

ClawfulGood
A "joey"? In your POUCH???

TURN PAGE

KoaltyTime
Only until she's six months old.
Then the pouch is just for feeding.

SolarBear
None of you are real
bears. I'm going to bed.

SolarBear has left the chat.

ClawfulGood
If he's sleeping during the day, he
shouldn't call himself a "sun bear."

HoneyHabit
Poser.

@red-capped_manakin

🎵 "U Can't Touch This" • by MC Hammer

Check out my signature dance move! When I start moon-walking along my branch, female manakins can't help but take notice. Some birds may call me a show-off, but I can't help that my feathers are so fly.

DANCE DANCE EVOLUTION

510

341

Dolphinstagram

coati
📍 Central America

 1,012 likes

coati Spread the word: Coatis rock. Groups of coatis are even called "bands" and are made up of females and our babies. We all have distinctive tails, long snouts, and double-jointed ankles. We have major star power; we're just waiting for our big break. #Tailfie #GirlBand

llama zon
the *BEAST* place to shop

crunchy treats

Termites

Extra Crispy! **Termites** BBQ

Extra Crispy! **Termites** CLASSIC

Extra Crispy! **Termites** SPICY

Stock up on these snacks!

CUSTOMER REVIEWS

★ ★ ★ ★ ★ **A satisfying treat!**

bat-eared_fox Verified Customer

Some types of foxes chow down on rodents and rabbits, but I'm all about the bugs. Seriously, I'm obsessed. Of all the delicious insects in the world, harvester termites have to be the best. They make up 70 percent of my diet. Not only are they flippin' tasty and packed with protein, but it's fun to just lick them up off the ground. Nature's candy!

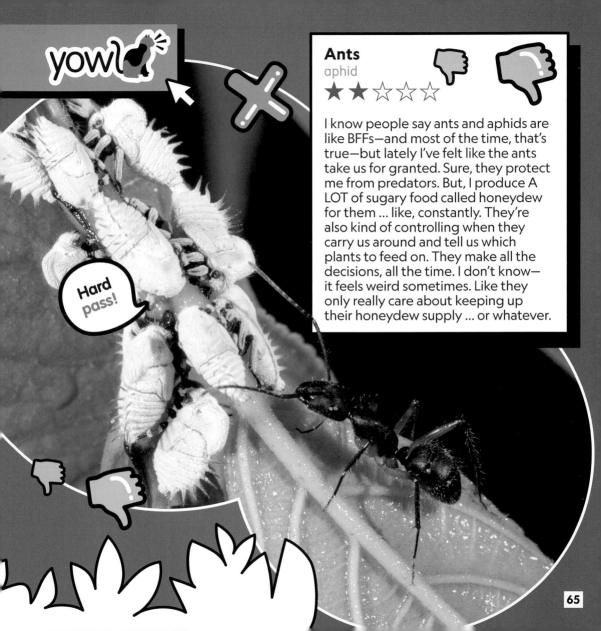

Ants
aphid
★★☆☆☆

I know people say ants and aphids are like BFFs—and most of the time, that's true—but lately I've felt like the ants take us for granted. Sure, they protect me from predators. But, I produce A LOT of sugary food called honeydew for them ... like, constantly. They're also kind of controlling when they carry us around and tell us which plants to feed on. They make all the decisions, all the time. I don't know— it feels weird sometimes. Like they only really care about keeping up their honeydew supply ... or whatever.

chipmunk
📍 North America

SELFIE!

💜 **103 likes**

chipmunk As requested, here are my answers to your chipmunk questions: 1) Yes, my stripes make me look cool. 2) Yes, it's true I can fit A LOT of food in my cheek pouches. Some say they can stretch to be three times the size of my head. 3) No, you cannot pinch my cheeks. #AskMeAnything

Home sweet home!

giant_wētā
Bay of Islands, New Zealand

We're back, baby! After a 180-year absence in the Bay of Islands, the "wētāpunga" are coming home. Shout-out to the Auckland Zoo, with support from Ngāti Manuhiri and the Department of Conservation. Thanks to them, more than 5,000 giant wētā have been released onto the islands. We're so happy to be back in our forest ecosystem—it has the BEST fresh leaves to munch on! We're paying it forward by producing extra-large insect poop, which helps fertilize the plants and spread their seeds.

Member for 2 years

Dolphinstagram

four-toed_hedgehog

Central and Eastern Africa

SELFIE!

 71 likes

four-toed_hedgehog Did you know that my "quills" are actually one-inch modified hairs made of keratin (the same stuff human nails are made from)? Adult hedgehogs have about 5,000 spines on their back and sides. If we get scared, we just roll into a tight ball and let the predator deal with some sharp pokes to the mouth! #SharpHairDontCare

KOKO
THE GORILLA

SPECIES
Western lowland gorilla

FAVORITE FOODS
Prunes, berries, and plantains

WHY SHE'S POPULAR
She could communicate
through sign language.

In her lifetime, Koko the gorilla learned to use more than 1,000 signs and understood 2,000 spoken English words.

Koko was born on the Fourth of July, 1971, at the San Francisco Zoo. Her full name was Hanabi-ko, which means "fireworks child" in Japanese. As a baby, Koko the gorilla was included in a research project in which she learned to use American Sign Language with researcher Francine Patterson.

When Koko was 12 years old, she asked for a cat. Researchers showed her a litter of kittens, and she chose a gray and white kitten that she named "All Ball." She was very gentle and playful with her kitten. She was allowed to care for a few cats as pets over the years.

Koko lived at the Gorilla Foundation's Woodside Sanctuary with two other gorillas, Michael and Ndume. Michael learned to sign as well, so researchers theorized that sign language could be a widespread form of communication for gorillas. During her life, Koko had a huge impact on the ways that people thought about gorillas, their abilities, and their potential to "talk" to humans in the future.

Gorillas share **98 PERCENT** of their **DNA WITH HUMANS!**

The exact number of western lowland gorillas is not known because they **INHABIT** some of the **MOST DENSE** and remote **RAINFORESTS** in Africa.

Western lowland gorillas are **SLIGHTLY SMALLER** than other gorilla **SUBSPECIES.**

CRITTER CHAT

BLUESPOTTED LAGOON RAY

SCREEN NAME: StingOperation
CHAT TOPIC: Venom Killers

FRIENDS

CreamPuff
Pufferfish

ShyGuy
Blue-ringed octopus

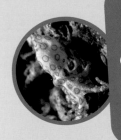

BodyShock
Blue coral snake

StingOperation
Chatting on my phone is the only place I feel comfortable. I'm such a #Introvert.

   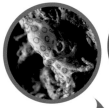 

ShyGuy
Same! I've been hiding out in a shell all day.

CreamPuff
Yup. I don't do well in crowds. If someone gives me the wrong look, I'm going to puff up REAL BIG.

ShyGuy
What do you do next?

CreamPuff
That's kind of it.

TURN PAGE

StingOperation

I've got a venomous barb at the end of my tail. If anyone bothers me, they get THE BARB.

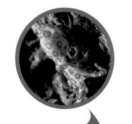

ShyGuy

My venom is a thousand times more powerful than cyanide! I use it to paralyze prey.

CreamPuff

Well, if you eat me, you'll ingest a powerful venom that blocks nerve signals.

StingOperation

Hmm, technically that sounds like poison, not venom, CreamPuff.

74

ShyGuy
Yeah, venom is injected but poison is eaten.

StingOperation
Plus, it's not very cool if you have to get eaten first.

BodyShock
Poor strategy.

CreamPuff
This is why I don't talk to anybody.

Dolphinstagram

marabou_stork
📍 Africa

 127 likes

marabou_stork Look, not all birds have to be pretty. My bald head and big beak allow me to reach into all those tight spots. By eating mostly decaying dead animals, I help speed up the decomposition process and prevent the spread of harmful disease. Someone's got to take out the trash! #LeftoversRule

bharmony

matches   profile   my photos

SuperSnackMan

SPECIES: Hanging fly
LIKES: Hunting, window screens
DISLIKES: Picky eaters, fly swatters, bug spray

ABOUT ME: My love language is gift giving! You won't leave hungry if you go out with me. I'm always prepared with crunchy arthropod snacks for my dates. I know all the best bugs, so message me if you'd like to meet up.

I never show up to a date empty-handed!

connect with me!

CRAFTY
COMMUNICATOR

African elephants

Although they can't use cell phones, elephants have other ways of staying in touch over long distances. Their super sensitive ears can hear a trumpet from six miles (10 km) away. If the elephants are farther away, they need their feet.

Rumbles—too low for human ears—travel underground, where distant elephant feet can detect them. Nerves in the elephants' feet send signals to the brain, which interprets the vibrations as sound, just like those picked up by the ear. Now that's some fancy footwork!

As highly social animals, elephants rely on sounds and body language to express comfort, friendship, aggression, fear, and even uncertainty. And even though they're led by a matriarch, or female leader, herds rely on group consensus to make decisions. Communication is key!

An **ADULT ELEPHANT** eats 300–500 pounds (136–227 kg) of **FOOD** a day.

An elephant trunk can **KNOCK OVER** a **TREE** and **PLUCK** a single blade of **GRASS.**

African elephants use their **TRUNKS** to **DIG THEIR OWN WATERHOLES.**

llamazon
the *BEAST* place to shop

sea lion accessories

Swim Fins

CUSTOMER REVIEWS

Thank you. Next!

★☆☆☆☆ **Don't take the plunge!**

California_sea_lion Verified Customer

These swim fins didn't fit, and I even lost one when I tried to bring my fore-flippers together in a sweeping motion called a clap. I swim by stretching my flippers out and then quickly tucking them against my body. I'm the only aquatic mammal that swims this way, so maybe these just aren't for me. That's OK with me. I'm already a natural torpedo!

Dolphinstagram

zebu
📍 Southern Asia and Africa

❤️ **42 likes**

zebu I learned so much visiting an art museum today! Did you know zebu have been domesticated since about 3000 B.C.E.? I saw quite a few ancient artworks depicting zebu. It's so cool to see how important we were to different cultures. #IAmAWorkOfArt

CRITTER CHAT

PANTHER CHAMELEON

SCREEN NAME: EyeSpy
CHAT TOPIC: Madagascar

FRIENDS

FossaPalooza
Fossa

FreakyFingers
Aye-aye

WingNut
Comet moth

EyeSpy
If you had to eat only one food for the rest of your life, what would it be?

FossaPalooza
Listen, I'm the largest carnivore in Madagascar. There's no way I'm picking just one food!

EyeSpy
If you HAD to, though.

FreakyFingers
GRUBS!!!

SELFIE!

FossaPalooza
Definitely not grubs.

TURN PAGE

WingNut
Please don't talk about food. I'm literally starving!

EyeSpy
What are you hungry for?

WingNut
I can't eat! I spent two months eating leaves as a larva, but adult comet moths don't have mouths or digestive systems!

EyeSpy
You are bumming me out.

FreakyFingers
I wonder what comet moth larvae taste like.

10:58 p.m.

EyeSpy
Maybe this was a bad topic. Should we talk about something else?

FossaPalooza
OK, I've got it. LEMURS!

FreakyFingers
Good idea! Lemurs (like me) are fascinating! #LemurClub

FossaPalooza
AND a delicious source of protein! #NomNom #Foodie #Yum

FreakyFingers
...

WingNut
No food talk!

YiPadvisor

Go for the nightlife!

solenodon
Havana, Cuba

🐾 🐾 🐾 🐾 🐾

Member for 73 million years

For my birthday this year, I finally left my forest burrow and treated myself to a trip into town. I'm nocturnal, so I really enjoyed the Cuban nightlife. Even though I can only waddle around, I loved all the dancing. And the music was great! It's too bad humans get all freaked out by my long, bald tail and musty, goatlike smell. I'm like, "Relax, human! I may be venomous, but I won't bite!"

yowl

Supermarket Produce Section
nectar-feeding_bat

★★★★★

I just had to post this review after visiting the produce section of the new grocery store that just opened. It was so satisfying to see all the different types of fruits on display: bananas, mangoes, guava, and so many more. As a nectar-feeding bat, I work really hard to help pollinate plants, and I just felt proud to see so many people buying these fruits to take home and enjoy. Hooray for chiropterophily! (That's a fancy word for pollination of plants by bats.) Yay!

You're welcome!

Dolphinstagram

pink_fairy_armadillo
📍 Central Argentina

 420 likes

pink_fairy_armadillo I'm only four inches (10 cm) long, I spend most of my time underground, and I'm nocturnal! People hardly ever see me! That's fine with me. I like to look my best even when no one's around to appreciate it. Have you seen my two sets of claws? I dig tunnels with them all day long, and they still look fabulous! #NailedIt #FashionAndFunction

CRITTER CHAT

WALRUS

SCREEN NAME: Tons_of_Fun
CHAT TOPIC: Full House

FRIENDS

MamaMandrill
Mandrill

That_Kat
Meerkat

Miss_Tunaverse
Albacore tuna

Tons_of_Fun

I'm at a beach party with hundreds of other walruses! Just found a moment to sneak away to chat.

Miss_Tunaverse

I totally get it. When I migrate, I'm with a school up to 19 miles (30.5 km) wide. It's fun swimming together, but sometimes I need an escape.

That_Kat

There's no escape when you're a meerkat! We live and hunt in big gangs. #FamSandwich

MamaMandrill

poop

TURN PAGE ● ● ●

93

Miss_Tunaverse
What are you up to, That_Kat?

That_Kat
My brother and I are stuck babysitting some kids right now while their mom is out foraging.

Tons_of_Fun
Sounds sweet, but I would never do that. Male and female walruses usually stay in separate herds.

MamaMandrill
u r a poo poo face

94

Tons_of_Fun
Is there a problem, MamaMandrill?

Miss_Tunaverse
She's usually not like this.

MamaMandrill
SORRY!!! That was all my DAUGHTER. I groom her, but I can't control her. LOL!

That_Kat
y does ur face look like that?

Tons_of_Fun
Looks like you're having kid trouble, too, That_Kat!

That_Kat
no i really want 2 know

BRONX ZOO COCKROACHES

SPECIES
Madagascar hissing cockroach

FAVORITE FOODS
Decaying fruits, plants, and animals

WHY THEY'RE POPULAR
They make a fun valentine!

At almost four inches (10 cm) long, Madagascar hissing cockroaches can seem pretty scary—especially when they make their famous *hisssssss*. But have no fear: They aren't poised to strike like a snake. Often, they're hissing to attract a mate.

The roaches' unique hissing sound is made by forcing air through breathing tubes on their abdomens.

They hiss to communicate in different scenarios. Male roaches will hiss during courtship and as warnings to other males. Males will also aggressively ram rivals with large horns that grow behind their heads and push with their abdomens. Love really is a battlefield for these roaches!

It's fitting, then, that these cockroaches have gained fame as Valentine's Day icons. It's all thanks to the Bronx Zoo. For a small donation, you can name one of their 10,000-plus Madagascar hissing cockroaches after a loved one as a unique Valentine's Day gift. Naming a roach may seem like an odd way to show that you care, but considering all these roaches do for love, it may be the perfect gift. Plenty of people seem to think so, too; the Valentine's Day tradition has been going strong for more than 10 years.

The **PADS** and **HOOKS** on their feet make them **EXCELLENT CLIMBERS,** even on smooth surfaces.

NINETY-NINE PERCENT of cockroach species do not inhabit human spaces and **ARE NOT PESTS.**

The **HISSING** is so **LOUD** it can be heard **12 FEET** (4 m) **AWAY!**

DANCE DANCE EVOLUTION

@honeybee

♫ "Fly Away" • by Lenny Kravitz

Waggle with me! My moves aren't just for fun. They give other bees directions! As a forager bee, it's my job to report back to the hive when I've found good feeding grounds. My "waggle" dance tells the other bees how far away the source is and even its direction in relation to the sun. The dance floor can get a bit crowded since it's inside the hive. But we honeybees don't let that stop the party.

420

42

llamazon
the **BEAST** place to shop

unruly beards

Comb and Barber Kit

I look good!

CUSTOMER REVIEWS

★★★★★ **GREAT GROOMING TOOL!**

De_Brazzas_monkey Verified Customer

This little gem has really helped me maintain my distinctive look. It glides smoothly through my long white beard. It was a little tricky to get the hang of, but now I wonder how I lived without one. No more pieces of leaves, flowers, or insects stuck in my beard! I just ordered more to give as gifts.

Dolphinstagram

wombat
📍 Australia

 1,012 likes

wombat I can't help but brag about my unique achievement—I'm the only known species that poops in cubes. I stack them in piles to mark my territory. The unique shape helps them stay put! #EveryonePoops #ItsNatural #CubePride

CRITTER CHAT

SPINNER DOLPHIN
SCREEN NAME: Clicker
CHAT TOPIC: Swim Team

FRIENDS

Herman
Manatee

Pinchy
European lobster

Flathead
Hammerhead shark

Clicker
Just did seven spins above the water and I am PUMPED!

Herman
Oh dear. I don't think I could manage ONE spin!

Clicker
Spinning removes pesky remoras and is one of the ways I communicate with my buds. Plus it ROCKS! *#Spinfreak*

SELFIE!

Pinchy
Who needs friends?

TURN PAGE

Clicker
You should try it, Herm buddy! Start with a slow, underwater barrel roll, then increase your speed to seven spins per second once you're above water.

Herman
I prefer to move about five miles an hour (8 km/h).

Flathead
I'm with Herman. Stay underwater so you can find food hiding in the sand. I've got electrical receptors in my head to locate sand dwellers. *#FoodGPS*

Pinchy
Whoa, that's amazing, Flathead! Hey, wait a minute.

Pinchy
Here's a hobby for you to try, Herman: molting. I do it once a year. My shell comes right off.

Herman
That sounds ... gross?

Pinchy
Not to me. Plus, you get to eat it afterward. It's full of healthy nutrients!

Clicker
Everybody try jumping and spinning RIGHT NOW! I guarantee it will change your life.

Herman
I think I'll just eat some seagrass instead.

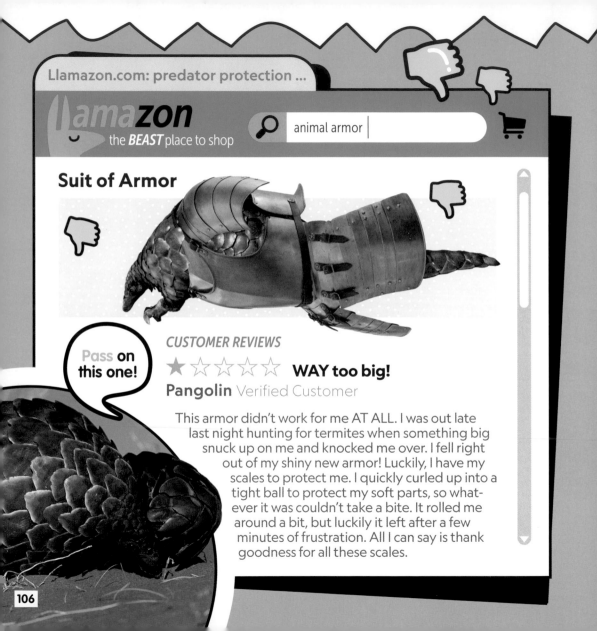

llamazon
the **BEAST** place to shop

animal armor

Suit of Armor

Pass **on** this one!

CUSTOMER REVIEWS

★☆☆☆☆ **WAY too big!**

Pangolin Verified Customer

This armor didn't work for me AT ALL. I was out late last night hunting for termites when something big snuck up on me and knocked me over. I fell right out of my shiny new armor! Luckily, I have my scales to protect me. I quickly curled up into a tight ball to protect my soft parts, so whatever it was couldn't take a bite. It rolled me around a bit, but luckily it left after a few minutes of frustration. All I can say is thank goodness for all these scales.

Dolphinstagram

satanic_leaf-tailed_gecko
📍 Central tropical rainforest, Madagascar

SELFIE!

 332 likes

satanic_leaf-tailed_gecko It's not easy to stand out in Madagascar ... and that's good! Blending in is all I want to do during the day. I spend hours just hanging off a branch like a leaf, or I can flatten myself against a tree for camouflage. Birds can't see me, so I'm off the menu!

SEABISCUIT
THE RACEHORSE

SPECIES
Thoroughbred stallion

FAVORITE FOODS
Hay and oats

WHY HE'S POPULAR
His spirit and determination

Seabiscuit was a popular racehorse during the Great Depression. He came from a family of racing champions, but he didn't seem to be of the same caliber at first. He didn't have a powerful body or an easy-going attitude. In fact, his first trainer called him "dead lazy."

But with a new owner, trainer, and jockey on the team, Seabiscuit surprised everyone with his speed. He started winning races, and the story of his underdog success spread throughout the country. One of his most memorable races was in 1938 against legendary horse War Admiral. People listened to the race on the radio and cheered when Seabiscuit won. It was called "The Race of the Century."

A few weeks after the big win, Seabiscuit suffered an injury to his leg. His owner and trainer took good care of him and helped him slowly recover. He was able to return to the racetrack in early 1940 for his last big win, and he set a new record with his performance!

There are currently **SEVEN STATUES** of Seabiscuit **AROUND** the **WORLD,** including one at his resting place.

Seabiscuit had a **COMPANION HORSE** named **PUMPKIN** to keep him calm and happy. Pumpkin was a palomino horse.

Seabiscuit wasn't always a champion. It wasn't until his **18TH RACE** that he finally won!

yowl

Herb Garden
ladybug

★★★★☆

Such a convenient place to grab lunch! I was so lucky to find one of these sitting out on a patio one summer. I'm a big fan of gardens because their plants often have little pests like aphids, mealybugs, and leafhoppers that I crave. So imagine my surprise when I crawled upon this lush buffet with flowers and herbs like cilantro, dill, and scented geraniums. I'll definitely be back!

YUM!

 **bharmony**

Tunneler_of_Love

SPECIES: Dung beetle
LIKES: Elephants, cows, and rhinos
DISLIKES: Cold weather, fresh food, dung thieves

ABOUT ME: I am a proud environmental activist. By moving dung around, I make the soil healthier. I also consider myself an animal activist, since I help protect cattle from pests like flies when I bury their dung. I'm looking for a strong partner who is ready to make the world a better place—together. Must love dung.

connect with me!

Let's roll!

111

CRITTER CHAT

4:32 p.m.

BradleyCougar
I always get jaguars and leopards confused because your spots look the same.

SpottySignal
That's because SOMEONE here is a total copycat.

HotSpot
Whatever! We look nothing alike. Jaguars have spots inside their rosettes, but leopards are solid.

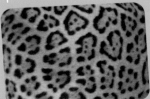

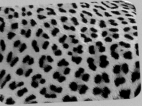

BradleyCougar
Still, you look more alike than, say, a black panther.

  SpottySignal
WHAT! Don't get me started!

HotSpot
Yeah, panthers have so many markings they look black. But they can be leopards OR jaguars.

BradleyCougar
OK, now I can't tell anyone apart.

TURN PAGE

FastClass
i'm here hi hi

SpottySignal
You're always running off!

BradleyCougar
FastClass, is it true your spots go down to your skin?

FastClass
something just moved in the grass gotta go

HotSpot
I don't know why she bothers.

Dolphinstagram

mountain_viscacha
📍 Andes mountains

SELFIE!

 332 likes

mountain_viscacha I'm feeling cute today. But—what am I saying?—I always feel cute! I look like a fluffy rabbit, but I'm actually a kind of chinchilla, so my fur is super soft. It keeps me warm at high elevations in the rocky cliffs and slopes of the Andes mountains, where I live with my HUGE family. Seriously—colonies of viscacha can have around 80 members living together. Can you imagine that much cuteness in one place?? I can. *#FullHouse #FeelinCute*

CRAFTY
COMMUNICATOR

tree-hopper

Treehoppers have been called "brownie bugs" because their pronotum (part of the thorax) expands up and over their bodies, making them look like little elves. Although they're silent to human ears, these bugs send secret messages through the trees!

As the treehopper shakes its abdomen, vibrations travel through its legs into a leaf stem. The sound moves quickly through the plant and can be detected by other treehoppers nearby.

Like many insects, treehoppers use their legs to decipher the vibrations they feel. Male treehoppers often send out messages to potential mates. But they also have unique patterns aimed at other males that seem to be saying "Hey! That's MY leaf, buddy! Move along now!"

Females send signals too, often to communicate with their offspring. Treehopper mothers stay near their kids to guard them against threats. If only one of the kids shouts "Mama!" the mother may not pay much mind. But if they're all yelling for attention, it could mean a predator is nearby, so she will hop back to them!

In Scottish folklore, a **BROWNIE** is a **HOUSE SPIRIT** that can be helpful or mischievous!

Treehoppers can be **GREEN, BLUE,** or **BRONZE,** and often have spots or stripes.

Treehopper **VIBRATIONS** can travel as far as **THREE FEET** (1 m) along a stem!

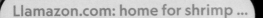

llama**zon**
the **BEAST** place to shop

🔍 punch-proof aquarium |

Aquarium

Too flimsy!

CUSTOMER REVIEWS

★☆☆☆☆ **Not tough enough!**

mantis_shrimp Verified Customer

I don't have time to tell you the full story, so here are the highlights: Yes, I have strong dactyl clubs for smashing and battering shellfish to bits. But did I *intend* to smash the aquarium glass and get the carpet all wet? No, I did not. What can I say? I am a force of nature. And this thing is flimsy.

Check it out!

pig-nosed turtle
Northern Territory, Australia

Member for 7 years

I just discovered a new estuary, and I'm in love! Northern Australia has so many warm freshwater streams, lagoons, estuaries, rivers, and swamps to explore. If you happen to see a turtle rowing with paddle-like flippers, that's me! I'm the only freshwater turtle that has them.

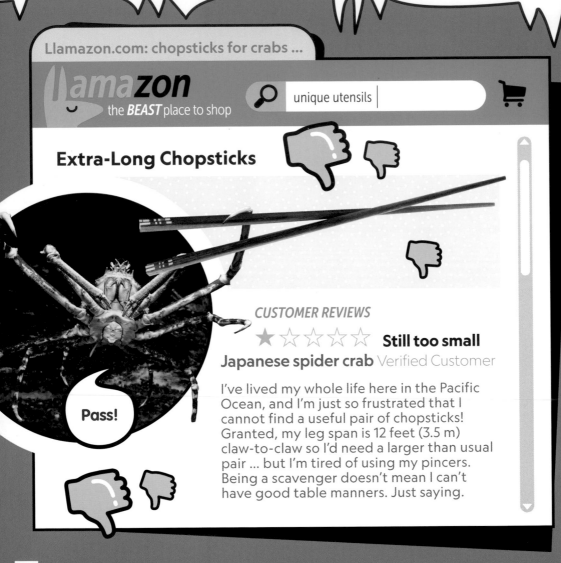

llamazon
the **BEAST** place to shop

unique utensils

Extra-Long Chopsticks

Pass!

CUSTOMER REVIEWS

★☆☆☆☆ **Still too small**

Japanese spider crab Verified Customer

I've lived my whole life here in the Pacific Ocean, and I'm just so frustrated that I cannot find a useful pair of chopsticks! Granted, my leg span is 12 feet (3.5 m) claw-to-claw so I'd need a larger than usual pair ... but I'm tired of using my pincers. Being a scavenger doesn't mean I can't have good table manners. Just saying.

Dolphinstagram

red-spotted guard crab
📍 Indo-Pacific

 420 likes

red-spotted guard crab This is an appreciation post for the small polyp stony corals I live on. We truly are BFFs. I work hard to keep my host coral clean and protect them against crown of thorns starfish. In return, they provide me with delicious slimy mucus to eat. *#ReefDefender #MoreMucusPlease*

CRITTER CHAT

JAPANESE MACAQUE

SCREEN NAME: Fresh_n_Clean
CHAT TOPIC: Foodie Friends

FRIENDS

SharpShooter
Archerfish

StoneCold
Egyptian vulture

Vlad
Northern shrike

...

Fresh_n_Clean

Just took a soak in the hot spring and am ready to unwind with some *#FoodieTalk!* Anyone try a new recipe or have any tips?

SharpShooter

I've concluded it's best to swim directly underneath your target for the most accurate shot.

Fresh_n_Clean

Target? I'm talking about food. I like over 200 different kinds of plants, and the occasional insect.

SharpShooter

Precisely. From my mouth I shoot a sharp jet of water up to five feet (1.5 m) in the air, knocking the insect straight down. Then I feast. *#BullsEye*

TURN PAGE
• • •

125

Fresh_n_Clean
Hm. That sounds a little complicated for me. One of my neighbors showed me that a sweet potato washed in salt water tastes so much better than one washed in freshwater! Any tricks like that?

StoneCold
You might think a buzzard egg or an ostrich egg is too large to open. But you can smash it over and over with a big pebble until it cracks. *#KitchenHacks*

Fresh_n_Clean
I'm not really comfortable eating someone's eggs, but thanks for sharing! What interests you, like, flavor-wise?

Vlad
The taste of a freshly killed mouse is exquisite. *#ChefsKiss*

Fresh_n_Clean
...

Vlad
I enjoy stalking mice, studying their comings and goings. But I also get a real thrill from hunting other birds. *#TheMostDangerousGame*

Fresh_n_Clean
OK. Just want to repeat, I'm asking for FUN foodie tips.

Vlad
Here's a good one: Don't let your food go to waste. Even if it's still alive, you can impale it on a spike to save for later. Anything sharp will do.

Fresh_n_Clean
Aaaand I'm out. I'll stick with my fruits and flowers.

127

golden_tortoise_beetle
⟟ North America

♥ **127 likes**

golden_tortoise_beetle I might not be as popular as my ladybug friends, but I'm just as stunning. Take a look at my shiny metallic gold coloring. Think of me as jewelry for the plants! *#BlingBling #WildStyleInspo*

bharmony

matches profile my photos

GalapaGirl

SPECIES: Blue-footed booby
LIKES: Sardines, confidence, beach days with friends
DISLIKES: Long walks, slippery rocks, tourists

ABOUT ME: This is my first time dating, so I'm a little nervous. I'm super excited to meet a potential bachelor who will flaunt his bright blue feet and dance to impress me. Offering me nice nest material is also important. Message me if you're in the Galápagos area!

Color me intrigued.

129

desert_locusts
📍 Northern Africa

SELFIE!

💜 **650 likes**

desert_locusts I'd like to set the record straight: We are NOT a bad omen. We just travel in swarms of tens of billions when we get the rare chance to chow down, like after a lot of rainfall. It's called a gregarious phase, and it's amazing!

131

Dolphinstagram

Mexican_mole_lizard
◦ Baja Peninsula, Mexico

 127 likes

Mexican_mole_lizard Even though I look like a worm, I have two forelimbs that I use to burrow into the dirt. I eat like a lizard—I love bugs like ants, crickets, and termites. I dig like a mole—I spend most of my time underground making elaborate tunnel systems. I'm like a lot of animals, but I'm also uniquely myself. #NotALizard #NotAMole #OutsideTheBoxAnimal

YiPadvisor

Where am i??

pygmy_jerboa
Camel ride in the Kharan Desert, Pakistan

🐾🐾🐾🐾🐾

Member for 2 years

As a native desert dweller, I'm always fighting for survival in the harsh elements. That's why I thought it would be nice to kick back, relax, and get off my feet for a while. I'll admit it was nice to see the world from more than two inches (5 cm) off the ground. But it WASN'T relaxing. Being on top of a camel's back just brought me closer to birds of prey that might want to swoop down and eat me! I couldn't wait to be back on the ground, near my cozy and SAFE burrow. Next time, I'll skip the camel and travel on my own two feet. That's fine by me: My hind legs are long, strong, and perfect for hopping across sand dunes.

CRITTER CHAT

BLUE MORPHO BUTTERFLY

CHAT TOPIC: Feasts of Color
SCREEN NAME: TrueBlue

FRIENDS

SirJumpsALot
Zebra spider

Beetlejuice
Dogbane leaf beetle

Tiny
Bee hummingbird

TURN PAGE

TrueBlue

Hey everyone! I'm chilling here on the forest floor and had to close my wings to get some camouflage. Too many hungry birds out right now. #TooBrightToIgnore

Beetlejuice

Yeah, I totally get that. I'm SO shiny with all my metallic gold, blue, green, AND red colors. I'm SO fortunate that I don't get eaten ... like, every day. #Blessed

SirJumpsALot

How do you stay safe then?

Beetlejuice

Oh, I use bitter and toxic chemicals called cardenolides to tell predators I'm not a lunch option. #StillLookingLikeASnack

TrueBlue

Must be nice to not worry about predators.

TrueBlue
Hey SirJumpsALot, I have a silly question. Are you really black and white or is that just a cool filter on your profile pic?

SirJumpsALot
That's my actual look! I'm a zebra spider so I get all that natural pop from my stripes. #BlackAndWhiteBeauty

TrueBlue
Cool, cool.

Beetlejuice
Yeah, I mean if you like ONLY two colors, or whatever.

TrueBlue
Um, you know I'm just ONE color right? #JudgeMuch

Tiny
Helllooo! I'm new to the group and just realized I'm the only bird. Is that OK?

TrueBlue
Of course! Welcome, Tiny!

SirJumpsALot
Yep.

Tiny
Thanks! It's funny, I'm often mistaken for a bee. I'm THAT small.

Beetlejuice
OMG, YOU ARE GORGEOUS! I'm SO jealous!

SirJumpsALot
Seriously!?! #SMH

137

Dolphinstagram

purple_frog
📍 Western Ghats of India

 94 likes

purple_frog It's that time of year again! Monsoon season, aka the few weeks each year I come out from underground. It's no wonder human scientists only discovered me in 2003. I may be mysterious, but my unusual color and pointed snout help me stand out from all the other frogs! #PignosedPride #OutsideTheBoxAnimal

 **bharmony**

TwitchyNose21

SPECIES: Eastern cottontail rabbit

LIKES: Running, jumping, eating gardens, hip hop

DISLIKES: Owls, crows, hawks, foxes, snakes, coyotes, raccoons, opossums, cats, dogs, cars ... I could go on and on.

ABOUT ME: I'm looking for someone young and adventurous. He has to be a really fast runner and also know the best spots for dense cover for safety. I prefer meadows and farmland, but I'm open to other locations for our first date. I've been practicing my courtship display, so he should be ready for my mighty punch to his ears and face! Kidding! (Not kidding.)

Love is a battlefield.

139

DANCE DANCE EVOLUTION

@weedy_sea_dragon

♫ "Dance the Night Away" • by Van Halen

Check out these smooth and graceful moves. I know I make it look easy, but it takes a lot of patience to get these steps right—and to find the perfect dance partner to "mirror dance" with. We have to be totally in sync as a couple. Like all great dance teams, timing is everything!

2k

42

Dolphinstagram

caribou
📍 Arctic tundra

 650 likes

caribou I know I say this every year, but I LOVE my antlers. They're great for defense and moving snow around to uncover hidden food. This year my antlers measured four feet (1.2 m) long. I'll drop my antlers in November and be without any until the spring. Sigh. Miss you guys already.

STARFISH
THE OPOSSUM

SPECIES
Virginia opossum

FAVORITE FOOD
Cashew nuts

WHY SHE'S POPULAR
Giving a (very cute) face to rescued and rehabilitated animals

Starfish the Opossum lost her tail when she was very young. Opossums have prehensile tails, which means they can grasp or hold objects. They use their tails for all kinds of important things, like collecting nesting materials and climbing. Without her tail, Starfish needed help to survive.

Fortunately, certified wildlife rehabilitator Ally Burguieres was ready to care for the young marsupial. She'd already rescued an opossum named Sesame, who had made a name for himself on social media. And today, Starfish is a star, too! She lives at Sesame's Bed & Breakfast in New Orleans, Louisiana, where she spends time with other rescued animals before they are ready to be released back into the wild.

Thousands of people watch on social media as Starfish and her companions play, rest, and grow. Although she can't be released back into the wild, Starfish lives a happy life at the bed and breakfast. There, she helps comfort other animals and teach people about how much skilled care wild animals need in order to thrive. They have unique nutritional needs and behaviors that often prove challenging for people used to caring for more common pets.

When in danger, opossums **PLAY DEAD.** They flop over, remain still, and stare for a long time.

Opossums are helpful! A single opossum consumes **5,000 TICKS** per season.

Opossums are the **ONLY MARSUPIALS NATIVE** to the United States.

Dolphinstagram

mata_mata
📍 Amazon rainforest

 420 likes

mata_mata Lately I'm all about the slow life. You'll most likely find me hanging out at the bottom of a freshwater stream, waiting for something tasty to float by. I blend in with the rocks and leaves, so fish are surprised when I suck them up and swallow them whole. #SlowLiving #FoodDelivery #VacuumUpYourFood #WhyChew

CRITTER CHAT

MARINE IGUANA
SCREEN NAME: Cannonball
CHAT TOPIC: Galápagos

FRIENDS

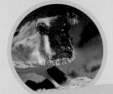

LipsDontLie
Galápagos batfish

BoobyTrap
Blue-footed booby

Rock_n_Rant
Flightless cormorant

Cannonball
Ah, what a day! You know that clear-headed feeling you get after a good swim?

LipsDontLie
I'm not much of a swimmer, but I love a nice long walk.

BoobyTrap
Oh sure, a swimming iguana and a walking fish.

Cannonball
Is there a problem, BoobyTrap?

BoobyTrap
Yeah, iguanas live on land. They don't swim.

TURN PAGE

Cannonball

I can dive more than 65 feet (20 m)! My long claws help me stay on the ocean floor for up to half an hour at a time!

BoobyTrap

I don't believe it.

Cannonball

You need to read a book!

BoobyTrap

I don't read fiction. *#OhSnap*

Cannonball

...

LipsDontLie
You're being trolled, Cannonball. Don't let them get to you. #DeepBreaths

BoobyTrap
And fish can't walk. You're not a real fish.

LipsDontLie
GET OUT OF HERE, BOOBYTRAP!!!

Rock_n_Rant
Galápagos batfish use their fins to walk along the seafloor.

BoobyTrap
LOL

TURN PAGE
• • •

Rock_n_Rant
How would you like it if we said birds don't have blue feet?

BoobyTrap
LOL

Rock_n_Rant
I'm being serious.

BoobyTrap
Oh, I know. When I try to cool down it just looks like I'm laughing.

SELFIE!

BoobyTrap
I'm real glad to see another bird. Let's fly outta here!

Rock_n_Rant
I don't fly.

Cannonball
Yeah, birds don't fly, BoobyTrap!

BoobyTrap
I mean, most do. That's why we have wings. Back me up, Rock_n_Rant.

TURN PAGE

Rock_n_Rant
My wings are for balancing on rocks.
You're making a nest of lies, BoobyTrap!

BoobyTrap
Whatever. I'm late for my date anyway.

BoobyTrap has left the chat.

 **LipsDontLie**
Hooray!

 **Cannonball**
You really can't fly, Rock_n_Rant?

 **Rock_n_Rant**
Nope. I jump!

llamazon
the *BEAST* place to shop

mask for migration

Filtration Mask

... and the search continues.

WARNING This respirator helps protect against certain particles. Misuse may result in sickness or death. For proper use, see supervisor or box. **N95**

CUSTOMER REVIEWS

★★☆☆☆ **Not a good fit**

saiga_antelope Verified Customer

Everyone knows the importance of a high-quality face mask these days. I thought this mask might help filter out dust and small particles during summer migrations, but it couldn't cover my sizable nose, and the straps dug into my ears. Good thing my nose already has closely spaced nostrils to help with filtration.

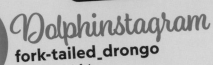

Dolphinstagram

fork-tailed_drongo
📍 South Africa

❤️ **127 likes**

fork-tailed_drongo I follow other animals and let them know if a dangerous predator is around. Sometimes I pretend something scary is coming ... then I steal the food they've abandoned in a panic. Hey, some scientists call it "kleptoparasitism." I call it a free lunch.

Slow_n_Steady

SPECIES: Land snail
LIKES: Flowers, vegetables, going out in the rain
DISLIKES: Heat, being in a rush, ducks

ABOUT ME: I'm just your average terrestrial mollusk looking for that special someone to share inside jokes, strolls in the rain, and, well, mucus. I haven't had much luck connecting with other snails through this app yet, since my response time is SO slow. But I'm willing to keep trying.

Escargot out with me!

connect with me!

CRAFTY COMMUNICATOR

prairie dogs

Near the exits of their vast burrows, prairie dogs watch for predators. A prairie dog is a favorite meal for hawks, coyotes, and bobcats. So whenever a potential predator is spotted, a lookout calls to the others.

A quick squeak means, "HAWK!" and sends everyone scrambling underground. But *chee chee chee* tells them it's a coyote. It means "Let's just be on guard and watch what it does." Prairie dogs have different calls for different predators, one of the few species in the world that appear to have "words" for specific things.

Prairie dogs even recognize a lot of variety in humans they encounter. According to Professor Con Slobodchikoff of Northern Arizona University, they seem to say things like, "It's that short human with the green shirt. She's walking pretty fast today." So if you ever walk by a prairie dog burrow, know that not only are they watching you—they could be gossiping, too!

Prairie dogs live in very **SOCIAL FAMILY GROUPS** and large "towns."

The largest recorded **PRAIRIE DOG TOWN:** 25,000 square miles (65,000 sq km).

Prairie dog **BURROWS** have designated nurseries, bedrooms, and bathrooms.

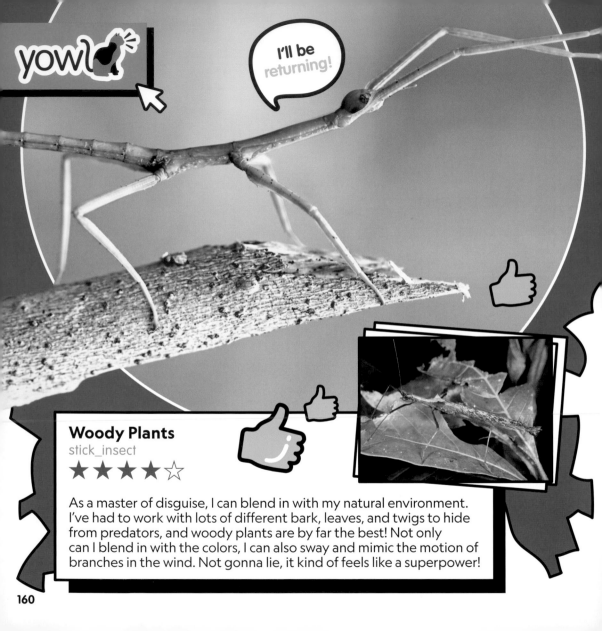

yowl

I'll be returning!

Woody Plants
stick_insect

★★★★☆

As a master of disguise, I can blend in with my natural environment. I've had to work with lots of different bark, leaves, and twigs to hide from predators, and woody plants are by far the best! Not only can I blend in with the colors, I can also sway and mimic the motion of branches in the wind. Not gonna lie, it kind of feels like a superpower!

161

llamazon

the **BEAST** place to shop

amphibian water sports

Beach Ball

It was **fun** while it lasted.

CUSTOMER REVIEWS

★★☆☆☆ **Cheap material**

Hairy frog Verified Customer

I bought this beach ball to toss around in the Central African rivers where I live. But it keeps deflating! That's not totally the ball's fault: Sometimes when I'm feeling threatened, I break my own bones to create claws that come out of my toe pads. Now the ball is full of tiny holes!

Dolphinstagram

honeypot_ant
📍 Southwestern United States

 225 likes

honeypot_ant All ants are essential workers in their colony, and I am part of the food management team. As a replete, I use my body to store food for future use by my fellow ants. My abdomen swells up like a balloon with sweet liquid. When needed, I can just throw up the liquid I've been holding so others won't starve. #Foodie

CRITTER CHAT

MUDSKIPPER

SCREEN NAME: SkipDay
CHAT TOPIC: Semiaquatic Kind of Life

FRIENDS

Satchmo
Trumpeter swan

PrettyCrabby
Land hermit crab

MissMoss
Vietnamese mossy frog

SkipDay

Society puts all this pressure on you: "Are you a land animal or water animal?" And I'm like, why can't I be both?

Satchmo

I don't know why we need to label everything!

MissMoss

It's easier to hide underwater. But let's be real. The cave is where all the roaches are. #FeedMe

PrettyCrabby

Don't you worry about snakes?

MissMoss

Nothing to see here, snake! I'm just a little ol' rock, covered in moss.

TURN PAGE

167

PrettyCrabby

I was born and raised in the water, but I've grown to love life on land. But SkipDay, you're a FISH, right?

SkipDay

I've got gills, but they don't define me. #OutOfTheBoxAnimal

Satchmo

Sorry if this is insensitive, but how do you *swim* on land?

SkipDay

I pull myself forward with my pectoral fins just fine, thanks! And my tail helps me skip and jump around.

PrettyCrabby

I've outgrown my old shell, and I'm on the hunt for a new one. Let me know if you see anything!

11:56 a.m.

Satchmo
I'm about to get airborne, but I'm nowhere near your neighborhood. Otherwise, I'd keep an eye out.

MissMoss
Have you tried searching on Zoolow for newly vacated shells?

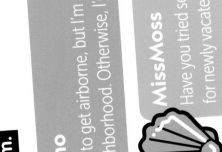

PrettyCrabby
Good idea.

Satchmo
I'm a big fella so I need a runway of about 100 yards (91 m), and I think I've got it. Chat soon!

SkipDay
Catch you on the flip-flop!

169

Peace and quiet, at last!

Malaysian mountains
giant_long-legged_katydid

🐾 🐾 🐾 🐾 🐾

It's pretty quiet here in the remote mountains of Malaysia. As the largest species of katydid on Earth, you might expect me to attract all kinds of attention from fans. But living here in the tops of trees I can avoid all that drama by blending in with the leaves and staying motionless. This lush green paradise gives me a safe place to just be my giant, long-legged self.

Member for 1 year

YiPadvisor

CRAFTY COMMUNICATOR

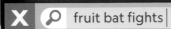

Egyptian fruit bats

If you spend time hanging with Egyptian fruit bats, one thing is clear: They're LOUD. Thousands of high-pitched shrieks echoing through the cave is enough to drive you batty!

"Get outta my way!" "I was here first!" After decoding many of their squeals, scientists have found four kinds of fruit bat arguments. They squabble over food, unwanted mating attempts, sleeping positions, or simply if another bat is too darn close. And just as you might change your tone when you're talking with a friend or a teacher, they squeal differently depending on which bat they're *bat*-tling with.

Baby bats learn the right squeals for the right situations from the colony they're raised in. Each colony has its own dialect, kind of like an accent. Anyway, why are you still reading this page? MOVE IT!!

Bats **CLICK** with their tongues, using **ECHOLOCATION** to navigate.

"Blind as a bat"? Nope! Bats **SEE WELL** in the **DARK.**

COLONIES can have up to 9,000 fruit bats.

Dolphinstagram

sea_hare
📍 North America

 222 likes

sea_hare I'm actually a marine snail with cute little tentacles that look like rabbit ears. I use these "rhinophores" to taste the water in search of algae and seagrass. Looking for my shell? It's on the inside! #FeelinCute #OutsideTheBoxAnimal

175

CRITTER CHAT

PUtiful
My scent isn't very useful. I just stink all the time. Food ferments in my gut and it causes me to reek.

SprayDaze
So cool. What do you smell like?

 **PUtiful**
Manure.

  Rank_and_Foul
COOL!

StenchKing
I got you all beat with the worst smell imaginable coming out of my butt.

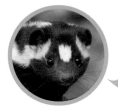

SprayDaze
Ooo, StenchKing is throwing down!

StenchKing
It's a thick slime called castoreum that horrifies every nearby nose!

Rank_and_Foul
Oh, wow!

StenchKing
No one alive can stand the smell of ... VANILLA!

TURN PAGE ● ● ●

PUtiful
Um. That doesn't sound bad.

SprayDaze
Vanilla smells good!

StenchKing
Oh, but it's a terrifyingly STRONG vanilla! #FerociousFunk

Rank_and_Foul
Still sounds nice.

Dolphinstagram

mangalitsa_pig
📍 Hungary

💜 **347 likes**

mangalitsa_pig I'm a domesticated pig known for my thick coat of curly hair. Kind of like a mix between a poodle and a sheep! It helps keep me warm during the cold winters so I can continue to enjoy the great outdoors. #ComfyCozy

@Olympic_dressage_horse

♫ "What Is Love?" • by Haddaway

Here's a throwback to my dressage performance at the Olympics. It's easy to get lost in the beats of cool electronic music. These competitions are all about rhythmic coordination between horse and rider. Trotting to the beat and cha-cha stepping takes a lot of practice. It sounds serious, but it's also seriously fun to watch.

420

42

DANCE DANCE EVOLUTION

CRAFTY COMMUNICATOR

splendid fairy-wrens

In Australia, a male splendid fairy-wren has a few strategies for finding and keeping a mate. He offers flowers, holding a petal in his beak as he fans out his cheek feathers. He dances for her, dropping slowly to the ground and bouncing upward in a "seahorse flight." But first, he often grabs her attention with a calculated scare!

Nearby, there are ruthless butcherbirds—predators who stalk, chase down, and kill fairy-wrens and other birds! When a female splendid fairy-wren hears the haunting call of a butcherbird through the trees, she listens. *How far away is it? Am I in danger?*

The male fairy-wren will join the butcherbird in a duet of sorts by singing his own birdsong in time with the predator. This makes a female fairy-wren more curious and receptive to the male fairy-wren.

Fairy-wrens make their nests with **GRASS** and **SPIDERWEBS.**

Fairy-wrens' predators, **BUTCHER-BIRDS,** impale their prey on a stick or thorn.

They are **NOT STRONG FLIERS.** They mostly forage, or "hop-search," on the ground or in shrubs.

Dolphinstagram

lilac-breasted_roller
📍 Kenya, Africa

 400 likes

lilac-breasted_roller Can you handle these colors? Count 'em— EIGHT slammin' colors. Even my feet: They're yellow with black tips. They call me the roller because of my steep dives during courtship. Like being on a roller coaster! And sometimes I rock back and forth, too. My voice isn't pretty but hey, that's rock 'n' roll. *ZAAAAK!*

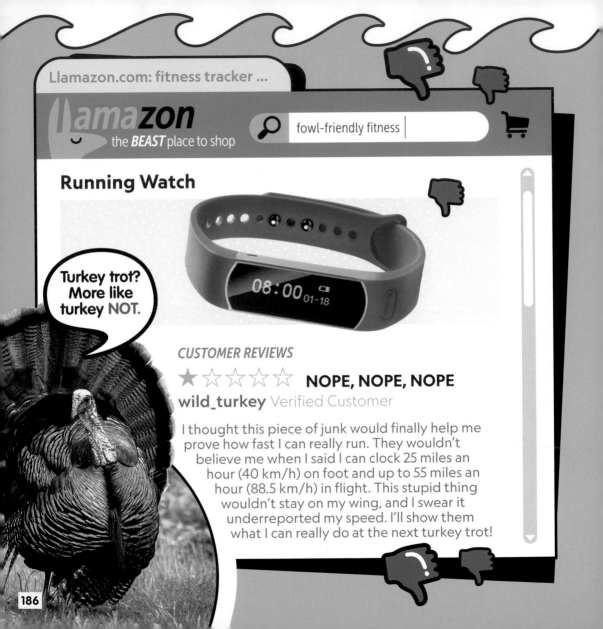

yowl

My Herd
yak

★★★★★

Just want to give a shout-out to my herd on the Tibetan Plateau! Hey hey! We live at the highest altitude of any large mammal and work together to find plants buried under the snow. We also stay warm at night and in snowstorms by huddling together with the youngest calves at the center. Winter temps of -40 degrees F (-40 degrees C) are no worry for us. We're really furry. Teamwork makes the dream work. Love you all!

12:30 p.m.

OinkoBoinko
Hey NobodysFoal, I read online that you're originally from Scotland! So cool.

NobodysFoal
Meh. My ancestors in the Shetland Islands used to work in dark, stuffy coal mines pulling heavy carts all day. #UnsafeWorkingEnvironment

OinkoBoinko
Hmmmm, well at least you inherited that healthy work ethic! I see little kids riding you all the time here at the farm.

NobodysFoal
It's true. They ARE heavy. How are they so heavy?

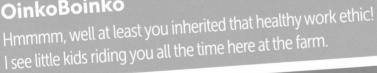

NobodysFoal
Hey, anybody interested in a quick swim? Sweating like a pig over here!

OinkoBoinko
Not funny! Pigs don't have sweat glands. *#Rude*

NobodysFoal
Sorry! I just thought maybe you'd like to wash off all that mud.

OinkoBoinko
Why do you think I roll in the mud? It's a great way to cool off ... and it really does wonders for my skin.

CombAlone
Self-care is so important.

TURN PAGE ●●●

CombAlone
Just got back from dust bathing with my flock, so I'm all good.

NobodysFoal
You don't use water either?!

CombAlone
Nope! We roll around in the dirt so the fine particles can clean our feathers of any lice or mites. Then we SHAKE IT OFF and preen.

OinkoBoinko
Well, now I'll have that song in my head all day! #Swiftie

@Andean_flamingos

♫ "It's Gonna Be Me" • by *NSYNC

It may look like we all came dressed the same, but the strength of your pink game is important in our group. You've got to be bright, and you've got to bring your best "head flagging" moves. A good head flag means stretching your neck and head up high, then turning your head side to side for dramatic effect. Our group display also includes marching and wing salutes to impress potential mates. Synchronized dancing never looked so good!

510

341

DANCE DANCE EVOLUTION

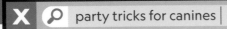

HARLSO THE BALANCING HOUND

SPECIES
Dachshund

FAVORITE FOOD
Treats, of course

WHY HE'S POPULAR
He can balance all kinds of things on his head.

It all started with a rubber chicken. In 2016, Harlso's owner, Paul Lavery, discovered the little dog could easily balance small items on his head. So they tried a little bit of every-thing to test Harlso's ability: a strawberry, a cupcake, a TV remote, a rubber duckie, a roll of toilet paper. He could do it all!

Mr. Lavery and his partner, Jen Scott, were so charmed by Harlso's talent that they decided to post pictures online. People quickly followed the account to find out what new item Harlso would have on his head next. Harlso often wears a bow tie to coordinate with the item on his head.

Harlso also likes to give back—according to his owners, money raised from his online presence has been donated to animal charities like Australia Zoo Wildlife Warriors, Dedicated to Dachs-hunds with IVDD, and Play for Strays.

The breed's name means **"BADGER HOUND."**

There's a lot of **VARIETY** in the **BREED:** Their coats can be smooth, long, or wire-haired, as well as lots of different colors.

The first **OLYMPIC MASCOT** was a dachshund named Waldi.

Dolphinstagram

mantled_guereza
⚲ Central Africa

 127 likes

mantled_guereza My coat gets me noticed everywhere I go! The long white hair on my sides and back create a dramatic fringe that really pops as I move through the trees. Takes a lot of leaves to keep this hair so shiny. And a lot of grooming sessions with my friends. #BlackAndWhiteBeauty #WildStyleInspo

LumberJack

SPECIES: Beaver
LIKES: Swimming, maple trees, keeping busy
DISLIKES: Sound of running water, vacations, dating

ABOUT ME: I'm a hard worker who is looking for my one true love. I've built a lodge that is move-in-ready, complete with a nursery and guest bedroom. I love big families and look forward to starting my own with the right mate. Serious responses only please.

connect with me!

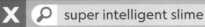

PHYSARUM POLYCEPHALUM

SPECIES
Slime mold

FAVORITE FOOD
Oatmeal

WHY THEY'RE POPULAR
They can solve problems without using a brain!

Slime molds grow on trees and forest floors. Technically they aren't animals at all—they're unicellular organisms that move a hundred times slower than a snail. That's SLOW. But even with no brain or central nervous system, they can still sense their surroundings. And scientists were shocked to see slime mold navigate mazes and escape from traps!

Through a network of pulsing veins, the slime mold nuclei work together to figure out the most efficient way to find the best snacks. When another slime mold approaches, they join together and teach each other what they've learned. After seeing this behavior, scientists couldn't help but wonder: What does it mean to make a decision? What is intelligence?

Hampshire College in Western Massachusetts added *Physarum polycephalum* as its first "non-human resident scholar" in 2017. From its office in the science lab basement, the slime mold sends letters to the White House offering its unique perspective on today's policy issues. Research assistants help with the questions, but the choices it makes are its own!

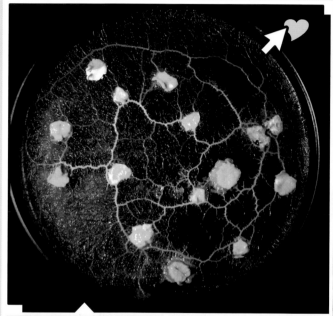

Similar to sea stars, slime molds can **REGENERATE.**

Like ants, slime molds mark the **PATHS** they **TRAVEL** so they can remember where they've been.

Bees, fish, and birds also display collective **"SWARM INTELLIGENCE."**

CRITTER CHAT

ECHIDNA

SCREEN NAME: DigginIt
CHAT TOPIC: Million Years Club

FRIENDS

SoShellLife
Green sea turtle

BlameItOnTheCrane
Sandhill crane

CowShark547
Cow shark

DigginIt
My feet need a rest after working on that hollow log demolition today.

SoShellLife
You mean you're not retired?

DigginIt
Gotta stay busy. Keeps me fed! And moving over 7,000 cubic feet (200 m³) of soil a year is good for the ecosystem.

SoShellLife
I'm about to turn 60, but I'm still mowing the seagrass every day.

TURN PAGE

CowShark547
You all think you're old? Cow sharks have been on the planet for at least 175 million years.

SoShellLife
Sea turtles are prehistoric, too. But that doesn't stop me from traveling more than a thousand miles (1,600 km) home every few years to lay eggs!

CowShark547

SELFIE!

BlameItOnTheCrane
Why did you send that?

CowShark547
Don't know. I just pushed a button.

BlameItOnTheCrane
The age of your species doesn't make YOU old.

DigginIt
Well, I sure feel old. I keep leaving comments on my son's Dolphinstagram, but he never writes back.

SoShellLife
Don't take it personally. Echidnas are solitary creatures.

DigginIt
Still, it's not too much to ask for a call now and then.

BlameItOnTheCrane
What's up with all the balloons?

DigginIt
What balloons?

YOU'VE REACHED **THE TAIL END** OF THIS BOOK. **WHERE HAVE YOU BEEN?** I've been waiting here **FOREVER,** but, well, to be honest I really only skimmed most of the book. I'm too fast! Now that our race is over, I've got to go back to the beginning and see what I missed. **Wanna join me?**

INDEX

Boldface indicates illustrations.

AS: Adobe Stock; ASP: Alamy Stock Photo; DR: Dreamstime; GI: Getty Images; IS: iStock; MP: Minden Pictures; NPL: Nature Picture Library; NGIC: National Geographic Image Collection; SS: Shutterstock

Cover (phone), Amnaj/AS; (cat), New Africa/AS; (zebra), Johan Swanepoel/SS; (paws), sonsedskaya/AS; Back cover (ladybug), irin-k/SS; (termite), bamgraphy/SS; 1, taboga/SS; 2, Stephen Frink/GI; 3, Charlotte/ASP; 4–5, Kandfoto/GI; 6–9 (wrasse), iSpawn/GI; 6–9 (parrotfish), Danita Delimont/GI; 6–9 (tunicate), paulreds/AS; 6–9 (giant clam), imageBRO-KER/Norbert Probst/GI; 8 (starfish), tae208/GI; 10 (UP LE), PabloBauza/AS; 10 (UP RT), Anastasiya Kandalintseva/GI; 10 (LO), DamianKuzdak/GI; 11, Michael Patrick O'Neill/ASP; 12, Paula Dillinger/ASP; 13 (UP), Kevin Kelly/GI; 13 (LO LE), Brian Wells/GI; 13 (LO RT), lucky-photographer/GI; 14 (LE & RT), Bernard Weil/Toronto Star/GI; 15 (UP LE), ZJAN/Supplied by WENN; 15 (UP RT), Bernard Weil/Toronto Star/GI; 15 (LO), ZJAN/Supplied by WENN; 16 (UP), Juniors Bildarchiv GmbH/R304/ASP; 16 (LO), Carl Jani/IS/GI; 17, Sahara Frost/SS; 18–21 (puma), Ondrej Prosicky/IS/GI; 18–21 (cheetah), mf795/IS/GI; 18–21 (jaguar), Freder/GI; 18–21 (leopard), Suzi Eszterhas/MP; 20 (jaguar swimming), Mark Newman/FLPA/MP; 21 (paws), Michael Cola/SS; 22, Cyril Ruoso/MP; 23 (UP LE), Stock Connection Blue/Dan Barba/ASP; 23 (UP RT), imageBROKER/Dieter Hopf/ASP; 23 (LO), Fallsview/DR; 24, Hira Punjabi/ASP; 25, Jurgen Otto/SS; 26–29 (skunk), Stan/AS; 26–29 (musk ox), Design Pics/Radius Images/ASP; 26–29 (hoatzin), Flip De Nooyer/MP; 26–29 (beaver), Kris Wiktor/SS; 29 (skunk handstand), Agnieszka Bacal/SS; 30 (UP), Amelie/AS; 30 (CTR), ksena32/AS; 30 (LO), Juniors Bildarchiv GmbH/ASP; 31, tracielouise/GI; 32, halamov/IS/GI; 33, Santia2/DR; 34–37 (rooster), Hemis/ASP; 34–37 (pig), Tierfotoagentur/J.Hutfluss/age fotostock; 34–37 (owl), Juergen & Christine Sohns/MP; 34–37 (pony), Rita Kochmarjova/AS; 36 (sideways owl), Anankkml/DR; 37 (rooster crowing), volodimir bazyuk/ASP; 37 (rooster), Toeizuza Thailand/SS; 37 (owl in barn), Juniors Bildarchiv/age fotostock; 38 (UP), Thrithot/AS; 38 (LO), GlobalP/GI; 39 (UP LE), Philippos Marakis/IS/GI; 39 (UP RT), David Fleetham/NPL; 39 (LO), Yoji Okata/Nature Production/MP; 40–41 (ALL), Jessika Coker; 42–43, Ken Kiefer 2/Cultura Creative RF/ASP; 44–47 (orangutan), Anna Baker/DR; 44–47 (shoebill), Edwin Giesbers/NPL/MP; 44–47 (wombat), Oll230/DR; 44–47 (pacu), Tracy King/ASP; 45 (durian), Noppharat05081977/IS/GI; 49 (UP LE), Mark Conlin/ASP; 49 (UP RT), Shane Gross/NPL/MP; 49 (LO), Maya Parfentieva/IS/GI; 50 (UP), kak2s/SS; 50 (LO), Manny DaCunha/AS; 51, Arcollette/DR; 52, Nick Taurus/AS; 53 (UP LE), Rixie/AS; 53 (UP RT), Villiers Steyn/SS; 53 (LO), Panoramic Images/ASP; 54 (sun bear with long tongue), 4FR/GI; 54–60 (tartigrade), Steve Gschmeissner/Science Source; 54–60 (kinkajou), Roland Seitre/MP; 54–60 (koala), Renate Micallef/DR; 55–60 (sun bear), jeep2499/SS; 58 (beehive), nicemyphoto/SS; 59 (koala & joey), myphotobank/AS; 61, Donyanedomam/DR; 62, GabrielPevide/GI; 63, Mary McDonald/NPL; 64 (jars), Dmitry/AS; 64 (termites), BEJITA/SS; 64 (LO), Jochen Dietrich/GI; 65, Morley Read/ASP; 66, Skyler Ewing/EyeEm/GI; 67 (UP), Ingrid Visser/Hedgehog House/MP; 67 (LO LE), Louise Murray/Science Source; 67 (LO RT), Fyle/AS; 68, praisaeng/GI; 68 (UP RT), MA Press, Inc./ASP; 69 (LE), Scott Smith/GI; 69 (RT), Danita Delimont/GI; 70 (BOTH), Ronald H. Cohn/NGIC; 71 (UP LE), Daniel Mears/Detroit News/AP Photo; 71 (UP RT), Anup Shah/NPL; 71 (LO), Michael Nichols/NGIC; 72–75 (ray), blickwinkel/Schmidbauer/ASP; 72–75 (snake), Eng Wah Teo/ASP; 72–75 (octopus), Michael Pitts/NPL/MP; 72–75 (pufferfish), Horizon/Universal Images/GI; 74 (ray tail), Alex Mustard/NPL/MP; 74 (octopus venom), Colin Marshall/MP; 75 (ray wings), maya_parf/SS; 76, Manoj Shah/GI; 77 (UP), blickwinkel/ASP; 77 (LO), Sabena Jane Blackbir/ASP; 78, Duncan Noakes/DR; 79 (UP LE), Anup Shah/MP; 79 (UP RT), AfriPics/ASP; 79 (LO), Anup Shah/MP; 80 (UP), BSANI/GI; 80 (LO), Alex Mustard/MP; 81, mihtiander/GI; 81 (inset), Gift of Evelyn Kranes Kossak, The Kronos Collections, 2015, Metropolitan Museum of Art; 82–85 (chameleon), kuritafsheen/GI; 82–85 (fossa), Nick Garbutt/NPL/MP; 82–85 (aye-aye), Chien Lee/MP; 82–85 (moth), Paul Starosta/GI; 83 (aye-aye eating), Albert Visage/FLPA/MP; 86, Yori Hirokawa/AS; 87 (UP), Eladio Fernandez/NHPA/Photoshot/Newscom; 87 (LO LE), Joel Sartore/GDA Photo Service/Newscom; 87 (LO RT), Grafissimo/IS/GI; 88–89, Tatiana Belova/AS; 90 (UP), MerlinTuttle/Science Source; 90 (LO), amphotos/ASP; 91, Science History Images/ASP; 92–95 (walrus), Paul Souders/GI; 92–95 (tuna), Natureworld/ASP; 92–95 (mandrill), Slowmotiongli/DR; 92–95 (meerkat), Vincent Grafhorst/MP; 93 (walrus on beach), Steven Kazlowski/NPL/MP; 95 (walrus flippers), Helene Sauvageot/AS; 96 (LE), barbaraaaa/IS/GI; 96 (RT),

Edward Westmacott/ASP; 97 (UP LE), kzww/SS; 97 (UP RT), barbaraaaa/GI; 97 (LO), Edwin Remsberg/ASP, 98, rtbilder/SS; 99 (UP), Kirill Skugarev/AS; 99 (LO), Floridapfe from S.Korea Kim in cherl/GI; 100, OII230/DR; 100 (inset), Suzi Eszterhas/MP; 101, FuYi Chen/GI; 102–105 (dolphin), Roland Seitre/MP; 102–105 (manatee), NaluPhoto/IS/GI; 104–105 (lobster), Sue Daly/MP; 102–105 (shark), Fred Bavendam/MP; 103 (dolphin leaping), Michael Nolan/robertharding/GI; 106 (UP), Natural History Media/ASP; 106 (armor), Halamka/GI; 106 (LO), AfriPics/ASP; 107, Paul Bertner/MP; 108 (LE), Archive PL/ASP; 108 (RT), KenWiedemann/IS/GI; 109 (UP LE), Michael Wheatley/ASP; 109 (UP RT), Archive PL/ASP; 109 (LO), Bettmann/GI; 110 (UP), mehmetkrc/AS; 110 (LO), Scheer Sieglinde/AS; 111 (LE), jacobeukman/IS/GI; 111 (RT), RainervonBrandis/GI; 112–114, (puma), Ondrej Prosicky/IS/GI; 112–114 (cheetah), mf795/IS/GI; 112–114 (jaguar), Freder/GI; 112–114 (leopard), Suzi Eszterhas/MP; 112 (jaguar spots), Pete Oxford/MP; 112 (leopard spots), 1001slide/GI 113 (black panther), Shaaz Jung/NGIC; 115, Mint Images – Art Wolfe/GI; 117 (UP LE), Tran The Ngoc/SS; 117 (UP RT), Oakdalecat/DR; 117 (LO), Husni Che Ngah/MP; 118 (UP), Solarisys/AS; 118 (LO), NaturePL/AS; 119 (UP), daniilphotos/IS/GI; 119 (LO LE), ZSSD/MP; 119 (LO RT), mikulas1/GI; 120–121, Hupeng/DR; 122 (LE), Pr2is/DR; 122 (RT), sommai/AS; 123, NPL/ASP; 124–127 (macaque), Fiona Rogers/MP; 124–127 (fish), Gerard Lacz/MP; 124–127 (vulture), Jose A. Bernat Bacete/GI; 124–127 (bird), Ronald Messemaker/MP; 125 (macaques bathing), online express/SS; 128, khlungcenter/SS; 129 (LE), Richard Walker/GI; 129 (RT), Renato Granieri/ASP; 130, Arterra/Universal Images Group/GI; 131, Stephen Dalton/MP; 132, Chris Mattison/ASP; 133 (UP), John Waters/MP; 133 (LO LE), Alain Dragesco-Joffe/MP; 133 (LO RT), Ghulam Hussain/GI; 134–137 (butterfly), SL/IS/GI; 134–137 (bird), Karine Aigner/MP; 134–137 (beetle), Paul Sparks/DR; 134–137 (spider), ErikKarits/IS/GI; 136 (spider from above), Ian Wilson/DR; 137 (butterfly wings), Hannamariah/SS; 138, NPL/Sandesh Kadur/ASP; 139 (LE), daveweth/IS/GI; 139 (RT), Claudio Contreras/MP; 140, Anky10/DR; 141, Donald M. Jones/MP; 142–143 (ALL), Ally Burguieres; 144–145, FuYi Chen/500px/GI; 146 (UP), ErsErg/AS; 146 (LO), Bethany Kays/GI; 147, Marina Giletich/DR; 148–154 (iguana), Steve/AS; 148–154 (batfish), Norbert Probst/GI; 148–154 (booby), Kirk Hewlett/ASP; 148–154 (cormorant), imageBROKER/GTW/GI; 150 (iguana on rock), petervanvuuren/IS/GI; 151 (batfish walking), Fred Bavendam/MP; 152 (booby calling), Adodi Photography/AS; 153 (cormorant flapping wings) Steve Roxbury/AS; 155 (UP), Lunx/SS; 155 (LO), Mikhail Gnatkovskiy/DR; 156, Jurgen and Christine Sohns/MP; 157 (LE), Iryna/AS; 157 (RT), NigelDowner/Science Source; 159 (UP LE), Peter Kirillov/AS; 159 (UP RT), Susan Rydberg/AS; 159 (LO), Gallo Gusztav/AS; 160 (UP), kuritafsheen/GI; 160 (LO), Atelopus/AS; 161, Jjustas/SS; 162–63, Gary Bell/Oceanwide/MP; 164 (UP), B.Trapp/Blickwinkel/age fotostock; 164 (beach ball), Chernetskaya/DR; 164 (LO), Paul Starosta/GI; 165, All Canada Photos/Wayne Lynch/ASP; 166–169 (fish), Pedro Narra/MP; 166–169 (frog), Michael Durham/MP; 166–169 (crab), Byrko/GI; 166–169 (swan), David McGowen/AS; 168 (fish on land), Earnest Tse/GI; 169 (fish fins), Pedro Narra/MP; 170, Suzi Eszterhas/MP; 171 (UP), Doug Schnurr/ASP; 171 (LO LE), Peter Yeeles/ASP; 171 (LO RT), Ravindran John Smith/GI; 173 (UP LE), Malcolm Schuyl/ASP; 173 (UP RT), Avalon.red/Anthony Bannister/ASP; 173 (LO), Steve Gettle/MP; 174, Jez Tryner/Blue Planet Archive; 175, Roland Seitre/MP; 176–178, (skunk), Stan/AS; 176–178, (musk ox), Design Pics/Radius Images/ASP; 176–178, (hoatzin), Flip De Nooyer/MP; 176–178, (beaver), Kris Wiktor/SS; 179, Elisabeth Eidjord/500px/GI; 180, dpa picture alliance/ASP; 181, Miroslav Hlavko/SS; 183 (UP LE), Wilf Taylor/ardea/age fotostock; 183 (UP RT), Ellgeemac/GI; 183 (LO), Andrew Haysom/GI; 184, Yva Momatiuk and John Eastcott/MP; 185, Joseph Mak/GI; 186 (UP), Marcelo Trad/IS/GI; 186 (LO), Vicki Jauron, Babylon and Beyond Photography/GI; 187 (UP), Alex/AS; 187 (LO), Daniel Prudek/ASP; 188–190, (rooster), Hemis/ASP; 188–190, (pig), Tierfotoagentur/J. Hutfluss/age fotostock; 188–190, (pony), Rita Kochmarjova/AS; 190 (rooster dust bathing), Krys Bailey/ASP; 191, Vladimir Seliverstov/DR; 192 (UP LE), Gene Rhoden/ASP; 192 (UP RT), LMPC/GI; 192 (LO), SteveByland/GI; 193, imageBROKER/Bernd Zoller/ASP; 194–195 (ALL), Paul Lavery; 196–197, Cathy Keifer/SS; 198, CraigRJD/GI; 199 (LE), Jillian Cooper/GI; 199 (RT), Richard Seeley/SS; 200–201, Oliver Wright/NPL; 202 (LE), Iuliia Morozova/DR; 202 (RT), MiraMira/ASP; 203 (UP LE), Naturalraw/SS; 203 (UP RT), Wirestock, Inc./ASP; 203 (LO), SergeUWPhoto/SS; 204–207 (echidna), pelooyen/GI; 204–207 (sea turtle), mekanphotography/AS; 204–207 (bird), LifeGemz/AS; 204–207 (shark), Doug Perrine/Blue Planet Archive; 206 (shark mouth), Michael Valos/DR; 208–209, mf795/IS/GI

For my family
—Jason Viola

Since 1888, the National Geographic Society has funded more than 14,000 research, conservation, education, and storytelling projects around the world. National Geographic Partners distributes a portion of the funds it receives from your purchase to National Geographic Society to support programs including the conservation of animals and their habitats. To learn more, visit natgeo.com/info.

For more information, visit national geographic.com, call 1-877-873-6846, or write to the following address:

National Geographic Partners, LLC
1145 17th Street NW
Washington, DC 20036-4688 U.S.A.

For librarians and teachers:
nationalgeographic.com/books/
librarians-and-educators

More for kids from National Geographic:
natgeokids.com

National Geographic Kids magazine inspires children to explore their world with fun yet educational articles on animals, science, nature, and more. Using fresh storytelling and amazing photography, *Nat Geo Kids* shows kids ages 6 to 14 the fascinating truth about the world—and why they should care. natgeo.com/subscribe

For rights or permissions inquiries, please contact National Geographic Books Subsidiary Rights: bookrights@natgeo.com

Designed by Mary Wages

Trade paperback ISBN:
978-1-4263-7371-8
Reinforced library binding ISBN:
978-1-4263-7593-4

The publisher would like to thank the book team: Kathryn Williams, project editor; Sanjida Rashid, art director; Lori Epstein, photo manager; Alison O'Brien Muff, photo editor; Katherine Kling, fact-checker; and Lauren Sciortino and David Marvin, associate designers.

Printed in China
23/PPS/1